SPILSBURY, Louise

The Islamic
empires

TIME TRAVEL GUIDES

THE ISLAMIC EMPIRES

EXPRESS EDITION

Louise and Richard Spilsbury

www.raintree.co.uk/library
Visit our website to find out more information about Raintree books.

To order:
 Phone 44 (0) 1865 888112
 Send a fax to 44 (0) 1865 314091
 Visit the Raintree bookshop at www.raintree.co.uk/library to browse our catalogue and order online.

First published in Great Britain by Raintree, Halley Court, Jordan Hill, Oxford OX2 8EJ, part of Pearson Education. Raintree is a registered trademark of Pearson Education Ltd.

© Pearson Education Ltd 2008
First published in paperback 2008
The moral right of the proprietor has been asserted.

Editorial: Kathryn Walker, Sarah Shannon, Harriet Milles, and Kelly Davis
Design: Clare Nicholas and Rob Norridge
Picture Research: Amy Sparks
Illustrations: Peter Bull
Production: Duncan Gilbert
Proofreading: Catherine Clarke
Originated by Modern Age
Printed and bound in China by South China Printing Company Limited

ISBN 978-1-4062-099-83 (hardback)
12 11 10 09 08
10 9 8 7 6 5 4 3 2 1

ISBN 978-1-4062-100-33 (paperback)
12 11 10 09 08
10 9 8 7 6 5 4 3 2 1

British Library Cataloguing in Publication Data
Spilsbury, Richard, 1963-
The Islamic empires. - (Time travel guides)
1. Civilization, Islamic - Juvenile literature
I. Title II. Spilsbury, Louise
909'.09767
A full catalogue record for this book is available from the British Library.

This levelled text is a version of *Freestyle: Time Travel Guides: The Islamic Empires.*

Acknowledgements
The publishers would like to thank the following for permission to reproduce photographs:
AKG p. **44** (Jean-Louis Nou); Art Archive pp. **13** (British Library), **15** (Topkapi Museum, Istanbul/ Dagli Orti), **18** (National Library, Cairo/Dagli Orti), **20** (Dagli Orti), **21** (Museo Correr, Venice, Italy/Dagli Orti), **25** (National Museum, Damascus, Syria/Dagli Orti), **30** (Dagli Orti), **40** (Bodleian Library, Oxford), **42** (Victoria and Albert Museum, London/Sally Chappell), **49** (British Library), **51** (National Library, Cairo/Dagli Orti); Bridgeman Art Library pp. **8** (Egyptian National Library, Cairo), **27** (Bibliothèque Nationale, Paris, France), **36** (Reza Abbasi Museum, Tehran, Iran), **53** (Museo Correr, Venice, Italy/ Giraudon); Corbis pp. **12** (Steve Raymer), **16/17** (Firefly Productions), **26** (Ed Kashi), **28/29** (Shepard Sherbell), **35** (Free Agents Limited), **43** (Kazuyoshi Nomachi/ Bettmann), **45** (Archivo Iconografico, S.A.), **46/47** (Nik Wheeler), **54/55**; iStockphoto pp. **6/7** (Paul Fisher), **10** (John Woodworth), **11** (Jan Rihak), **19** (Jane Norton), **24** (Matej Michelizza), **33** (Simon Gurney), **37** (Christine Rondeau), **38/39** (Jim Lopes), **59** (Damir Cudic); Werner Forman p. **41** (Werner Forman Archive/Alhambra Museum, Granada).

Background cover photograph of the Dome of the Rock, Jerusalem, reproduced with permission of Brand X Pictures. Inset photograph of gold deer from Cordoba reproduced with permission of Corbis. Inset photograph of tile reproduced with permission of the Bridgeman Art Library.

The publishers would like to thank Professor Timothy Insoll for his assistance in the preparation of this book.

CONTENTS

Words that appear in the text in bold, **like this**, are explained in the glossary.

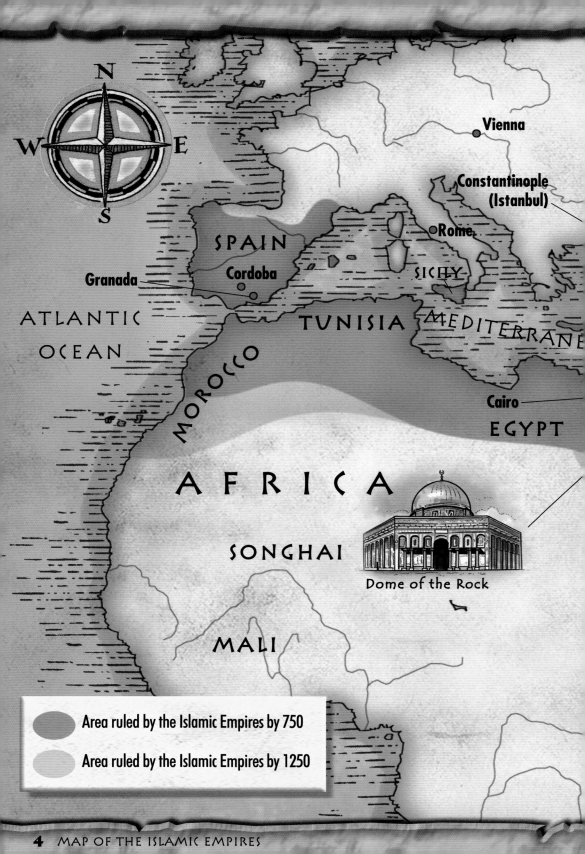

N

W · E

S

Vienna

Constantinople
(Istanbul)

SPAIN

Granada

Cordoba

Rome

SICILY

ATLANTIC
OCEAN

TUNISIA

MEDITERRANE

MOROCCO

Cairo

EGYPT

AFRICA

SONGHAI

Dome of the Rock

MALI

Area ruled by the Islamic Empires by 750

Area ruled by the Islamic Empires by 1250

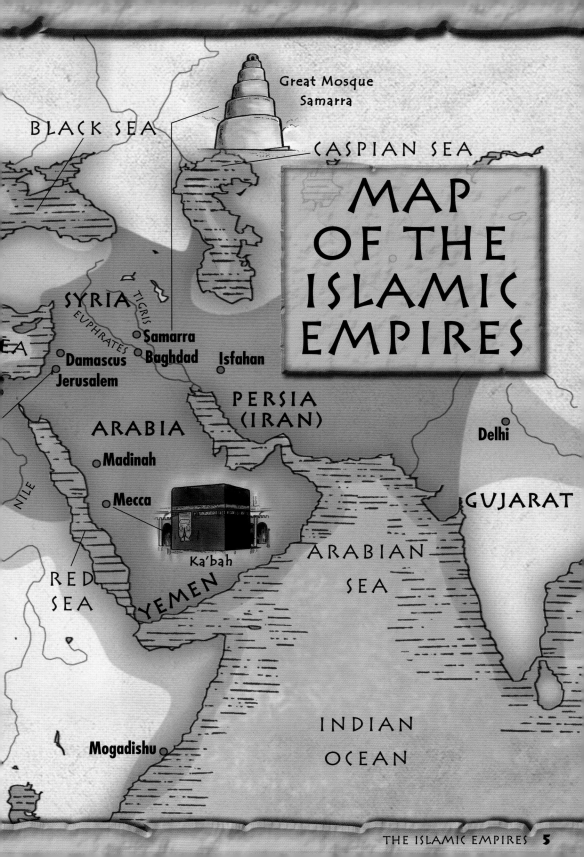

Great Mosque
Samarra

BLACK SEA

CASPIAN SEA

MAP OF THE ISLAMIC EMPIRES

SYRIA

EUPHRATES

TIGRIS

Samarra

Damascus

Baghdad

Isfahan

Jerusalem

PERSIA
(IRAN)

ARABIA

Delhi

Madinah

NILE

Mecca

GUJARAT

Ka'bah

RED
SEA

YEMEN

ARABIAN
SEA

Mogadishu

INDIAN
OCEAN

This beautiful building is called the Dome of the Rock. It is an important **mosque** in the city of Jerusalem. A mosque is a Muslim place of worship.

CHAPTER 1

FACTS ABOUT THE ISLAMIC EMPIRES

Welcome to the big, exciting world of the Islamic Empires. These are the lands controlled by **Muslim** rulers. Muslims are followers of the religion of **Islam**. They follow the teachings of the **Prophet Muhammad**. Muslims believe that the Prophet was the messenger of **Allah** (God).

The Islamic Empires cover a huge area. They also cover a very long period in history. This section tells you the best and worst times to visit. It tells you about the weather and the different landscapes. It also has some important information about the Muslim way of life.

WHEN TO VISIT

The religion of **Islam** began about 1,400 years ago. It began in the city of **Mecca**. Mecca was in Arabia (see map on page 5). In modern times it is in the country of Saudi Arabia. Many people became followers of Islam. They are called **Muslims**.

EXPANSION

The Islamic world grew steadily bigger. It was ruled by men known as **caliphs**. Caliphs were not only rulers. They were religious leaders as well.

The first major Islamic Empire started in AD 661, almost 1,350 years ago. It was called the **Umayyad** Empire.

Fifty years later, the Umayyad Empire stretched from Spain in the west to Afghanistan in the East.

This picture shows a Muslim army in battle. Some people were forced to become Muslims. This was when Muslim armies took control of their land.

GOLDEN AGE

The best time to visit the Islamic Empires is between AD 750 and 1258. That's between 750 and 1,260 years ago. This is called the Golden Age of Islam. During this time, the caliphs helped spread new ideas throughout their lands. They encouraged people to invent (create) new devices and better ways of doing things.

GOOD AND BAD TIMES TO VISIT

AD 610	The Angel Jibril (Gabriel) appears to the **Prophet Muhammad**. The Prophet turns to the religion of Islam.
622	Muhammad and his followers are chased out of the city of Mecca.
632	Prophet Muhammad dies.
661	**Umayyad** Empire begins.
750	**Abbasid** Empire begins.
762	Baghdad becomes capital of the Islamic Empires.
750–1258	Period often known as the Golden Age of Islam.
800–900	Muhammad's sayings and teachings are collected together.
836	Capital of Islamic Empires moves to the city of Samarra. This follows trouble in Baghdad.
892	Capital returns to Baghdad.
1095–1291	Muslims and Christians fight for control of lands. These wars are called the **crusades**.
1258	**Mongols** (people from central Asia) attack Baghdad. Abbasid rule comes to an end.

Key:

Stay away   Interesting times to visit   Best times to visit

LANDSCAPE AND CLIMATE

During the Golden Age (see page 9), the Islamic Empires stretch across many different landscapes. There are high cold mountains and warm coasts.

But most of the lands are in North Africa and western Asia. The weather there is hot and dry. You'll find deserts full of sand dunes and rocks.

HOT AND COLD

The desert offers little shade from the burning sun. But the nights can be freezing cold. The Sahara desert (below) covers a huge area of North Africa. Winds here can blow for days at a time.

RIVERS AND MARSHES

Many cities and towns in the Islamic Empires are built
near water. The city of Baghdad (see map page 5) is
built where two major rivers meet. The city of Cairo is
on the River Nile. Crops and fruit trees grow around
the rivers. Their waters are busy with boats.

There is a huge marshy area south of Baghdad. The
land is wet and soft. people who live here are called
the Marsh Arabs. They cut down the reeds that grow
in the mud. Then they weave the reeds together to
make floating villages.

ISLAMIC RELIGION

Muslims are followers of the religion of Islam. They believe that the **Prophet Muhammad** received **Allah's** (God's) word. A prophet is a messenger of God.

When the Prophet first told people about this, some of them became angry. He and his followers were forced out of the city of **Mecca** (see page 8). They moved north to the city of Madinah.

Many did follow Muhammad's teachings. This became the religion of Islam. The teachings are written in the **Qur'an**. This is the Muslim holy book. There are Five Pillars or duties that Muslims must follow.

Muslims must pray facing in the direction of Mecca.

THE FIVE PILLARS

The Five Pillars are:

1. Shahadah. This is saying that you believe in Islam. You will often see or hear the words "There is no God but Allah and Muhammad is the Messenger of Allah."
2. Prayer. All Muslims pray five times each day.
3. Charity. This means giving money to people in need.
4. Fasting. This means going without food or drink. For one month each year Muslims fast during daylight hours.
5. The Hajj. This is a journey to the to the holy city of Mecca. All Muslims try to make a hajj once in their lifetimes.

People who are not Muslims don't need to follow the five pillars. But they will still be welcome in the Islamic Empires.

This picture shows Muslims who have journeyed to Mecca. They are gathered around the **Ka'bah**. This is the most important holy building for Muslims.

WHO'S WHO IN THE ISLAMIC WORLD?

People in the Islamic Empires belong to different classes or levels. At the top are the **caliphs** and **sultans**. Caliphs are religious leaders who are also rulers. Sultans are kings who rule specific areas.

Next are military leaders. Below them come people who work for the government. The government is the group of people who run the country.

Merchants and traders are people who buy and sell goods for a living. They are usually well-off. Most ordinary men work as farmers.

At the lowest level are those who do dirty jobs. Below them are slaves. These are people who have been captured from foreign lands.

SPECIAL SLAVES

Mamluks are special slaves. They are trained to be private soldiers. They are also trained to be advisers for caliphs and sultans.

Some mamluks become very powerful rulers. For example, Salah ad-Din was a mamluk. He became a famous leader of Islamic armies.

WOMEN AND CHILDREN

Most women look after the home and children. Girls don't usually go to school. They learn how to run the home. Girls usually marry aged about 12 or 13.

Boys might look after animals or work in the fields. Some go to the **madrassah**. This is a school where they learn about their religion.

This picture shows a family travelling to the holy city of **Mecca**. They have stopped in the desert. You can see the mother and child in a tent. ↘

These camels are moving through the desert. Travelling by camel is the best way to cross these huge and lonely places.

CHAPTER 2

ON THE MOVE

Before you set off on your adventures, there are some things you really need to know about. In the Islamic Empires you can get into real trouble by wearing the wrong clothes. Making the wrong gestures can also cause big problems.

You may be travelling very long distances in the empires. Then you'll need to know the ups and downs of camel travel! Being a traveller here can also be dangerous. Many die from thirst or hunger. Some die from being too long in the Sun.

GETTING AROUND

You will see lots of travellers in the Islamic Empires. Students travel to Baghdad to study. People make their way to and from **Mecca** (see page 8). Some are always moving from place to place. These people are called **nomads**.

BY LAND

Many people travel by horse or donkey. But camels are the only animals that can go long distances without water. You see lines of up to 2,000 camels travelling across the empires. These are known as camel **caravans**. They are carrying goods such as salt and gold.

This map is about 900 years old. It shows the towns of Madinah (top) and Mecca (bottom).

BY SEA

For some journeys you'll need to travel on a **dhow**. A dhow is a trading ship used by **Muslims**. It is a type of ship used for carrying goods. You could pay for your journey by working on board.

Sea travel can be dangerous. Ships may be wrecked by storms. Also, there are many pirates at sea. They rob and kill people on board ships.

TRAVELLER'S TIPS
- Bring snacks. Many travellers eat dried fruits and nuts.
- Bring a cushion for a camel trip. Camels rock from side to side as they walk.
- Camel travel is slow. You'll only cover about 40 kilometres (25 miles) a day at most.
- Dried camel droppings are good for making camp fires.

WHERE TO STAY

Muslims are kind and welcoming to travellers. It should be easy to find places to stay on your travels.

IN TOWNS AND CITIES

In towns or cities someone will probably offer you a bed for free in their home. You might also be able to stay at a **mosque** (place of worship). Mosques often have sleeping quarters. These are meant for Muslims travelling to a holy place.

Homes in the Islamic Empires come in different sizes and styles. But a typical Muslim home has a courtyard. This is an open space in the middle. Indoors there are usually colourful rugs and low couches.

OUT OF BOUNDS

Homes are separated into men's and women's sections. The women's section is called the harem. Men are not allowed in.

This is a place where travellers can pray. It is at the centre of a caravanserai courtyard.

IN THE COUNTRYSIDE

Outside the towns, you should look for a **caravanserai**. These are roadside inns. They are places where **caravans** (see page 18) can stop and rest.

This picture shows a caravanserai scene. People are relaxing and chatting. Their animals are resting.

Each caravanserai is built around a large courtyard. You leave your camels, horses, or donkeys in the courtyard. Caravanserais have bedrooms and baths for the travellers.

WHAT TO WEAR

In most parts of the empires, wearing the wrong clothes can get you into trouble. People believe that **Allah** (God) wants them to be modest. This means not showing off their bodies.

WOMEN'S WEAR

Girls and women must cover up when in public. They should wear long, loose robes. Or they may wear a tunic over baggy trousers.

Girls and women should also wear a veil. You pull the veil across your face when you're out.

✔ This is the type of clothes worn by women in the Islamic Empires. A woman's robe should cover her ankles.

MEN'S FASHION TIPS

Men should wear long loose shirts and baggy trousers. They also wear a piece of cloth as a cloak. In some places men wear a turban. This is a long piece of cloth wound around the head.

The **Qur'an** (Muslim holy book) tells men not to wear silk clothes or gold jewellery. If you do, people will think you're a big show-off.

This man is wearing a tunic and turban. Most men dressed like this during the Golden Age of the Islamic Empires (see page 9).

FOOD AND DRINK

You will find lots of healthy and delicious food in the Islamic Empires. There are figs and oranges. There are olives and flat breads. Sheep's milk and goats' milk are used to make yoghurt and cheese.

You can get sweet pastries made with honey and sugar. People use spices to flavour foods. They use flavourings such as cinnamon and cumin.

WATERING THE LAND

Muslim farmers build canals and water wheels. These carry or collect water. Then farmers can water crops in the dry lands.

These are some of the spices used for cooking. They are sold in many markets in the Islamic Empires. >

This picture shows cooks preparing for a large meal. One cook (top left) is making bread. The others are stirring pots of meat.

MEATY MEALS

Eating pork is forbidden. You can eat other types of meat. But the meat must be **halal**. This means that the animals have been killed in a way that causes them least suffering. Islamic law says people should be kind to all creatures.

DRINKS

In the cities there are fountains of fresh drinking water. As soon as you arrive at someone's house you will be offered a drink. This might be a sweet mint tea. It might be juice made with lemons and sugar.

CUSTOMS AND BELIEFS

Many important **Muslim** customs are to do with the **mosque** (Muslim place of worship). All worshippers take off their shoes at the door. They wash themselves in a fountain or pool there. They do this to make themselves pure and clean before worshipping.

Inside, all the men sit on the floor. This is a sign that they are all equal to **Allah** (God). Women must pray in a different part of the mosque. But often they pray at home instead.

These modern Muslims are washing before entering a mosque.

MARRIAGE CUSTOMS

Marriages are arranged by parents. A couple often do not meet until their wedding day. Muslim wedding celebrations usually last for days. There is music, singing, and fine food.

FESTIVAL CUSTOMS

Muslim festivals are serious religious occasions. But they are also public holidays. **Ramadan** is a month of **fasting** (see page 13). The end of Ramadan is marked by Eid al Fitr. This is a three-day festival. People feast and give each other gifts.

This picture shows people marking the end of Ramadan. This is a time of great celebration across the Islamic Empires.

MIND YOUR MANNERS!

- Always wash your hands before sitting down to a meal.
- When seated, never point the soles of your feet towards another person. It is very rude to do this.
- There are no knives and forks. You must eat only with your right hand.
- Only use your right hand to shake hands with someone. It is extremely rude to use the left.

This remarkable spiral tower is part of the Great Mosque of Samarra. It is a must-see for visitors to the Islamic Empires. Samarra is a city in modern-day Iraq.

CHAPTER 3

SIGHTSEEING

There are some amazing sights in the Islamic Empires. Palaces are decorated with precious materials such as gold and jade. The **mosques** (Muslim places of worship) are places of great beauty and peace. The newly built city of Baghdad also has zoos and museums to visit.

BAGHDAD

The city of Baghdad (see map on page 5) is one of the top attractions in the Islamic Empires. It was completed in AD 762. That's almost 1,250 years ago.

Ancient Baghdad is bursting with beautiful buildings. This is the tomb of a ruler's wife. It was built about 800 years ago.

CIRCULAR CITY

Baghdad is a round city. It is surrounded by a set of thick circular walls. Inside there is a second circle of walls.

Baghdad is a rich and colourful place. It has libraries and museums. It has zoos and gardens. The city also has some of the most delicious food in the world.

A TOUR OF THE CITY

Follow these directions for an interesting tour of Baghdad.

1. Start outside the city walls. Follow the busy markets to the moat. This is a wide ditch filled with water.

2. Cross the moat and enter through one of the city's four gates. Inside are streets packed with small houses. This is where the poorer people live.

3. Towards the centre the streets are wider. They are lined with shops and large houses. Be sure to visit the House of Wisdom. This is a world-famous place of learning.

4. Next you reach a second set of city walls. Inside you'll find the grand **mosque** and royal palace.

PALACES AND FORTRESSES

While you're travelling in the empires, be sure to visit some palaces. These are huge buildings. They are built for rulers or other important people. A typical palace houses the owner and his many wives. It also houses his servants and soldiers.

SHOWING OFF WEALTH

Rulers like to show off their wealth. Rooms are often lined with beautiful stone or wood. In the palace gardens you can wander among shady plants and fountains. Some rulers even have zoos in their palaces.

THE CITADEL OF ALEPPO

There are lots of fortresses across the Islamic Empires. Fortresses are very strong buildings. They are designed to keep out attackers. One of the best fortresses to visit is the Citadel of Aleppo. This is in Syria (see map on page 5).

THE HALL OF THE TREE

In the **sultan's** (king's) palace in Baghdad is the Hall of the Tree. This is where you will see a tree made of gold and silver. The tree is full of chirping, mechanical birds.

This is the Citadel of Aleppo. It is built high on a hill. It overlooks flat lands all around.

MOSTLY MOSQUES

On your travels, you could visit some of the holiest places in the Islamic Empires. These are where Muhammad spent his life. The **Ka'bah** in **Mecca** (see page 13) is the most important of these. There is also the **mosque** in nearby Madinah. It is built over the place where Muhammad is buried.

THE DOME OF THE ROCK

In Jerusalem you can see the Dome of the Rock. This beautiful building is topped with a golden dome. There is a picture of it on pages 6–7.

Inside this building is a rock. **Muslims** believe this is where Muhammad went up to **Allah** (God) in Heaven.

WHAT'S WHAT IN A MOSQUE?

Here are some of the things you'll find in a mosque.

Minaret: A tall, slender tower. A person called a muezzin climbs the minaret to call people to prayer.

Mihrab: A hollow in the wall. It reminds worshippers which way Mecca is.

Minbar: A raised seat or platform. The imam is the person who leads prayers in the mosque. He speaks from the minbar.

THE GREAT MOSQUE AT CORDOBA

In the 8th century, most of Spain came under Muslim rule. That was about 1,300 years ago. Cordoba became its capital.

At Cordoba you can see the magnificent Great Mosque. Inside it is a huge hall. Hundreds of striped double arches support the roof.

This is the Great Mosque of Cordoba. It was built large enough for all the city's Muslims to meet in prayer.

DECORATIVE DESIGNS

Many Islamic buildings and objects are decorated with writing. This beautiful writing is called **calligraphy**. You will see it on **mosques** and palaces. It is also used on plates and in books.

Calligraphy on buildings may be carved into the stone or brick. It may also be painted on tiles. These tiles are cemented onto the building.

BEAUTIFUL GEOMETRY

Throughout the empires you will also see lots of geometric patterns. These are patterns made with shapes such as squares, circles, or triangles. The shapes are repeated and linked together in interesting ways.

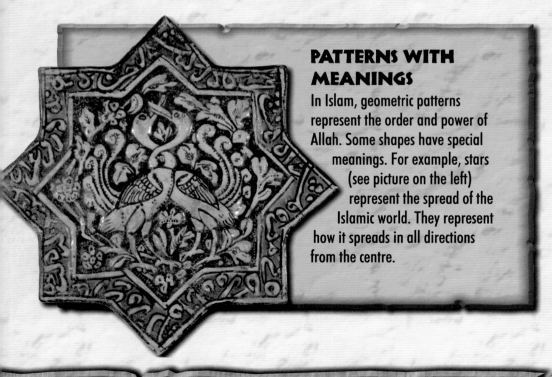

PATTERNS WITH MEANINGS

In Islam, geometric patterns represent the order and power of Allah. Some shapes have special meanings. For example, stars (see picture on the left) represent the spread of the Islamic world. They represent how it spreads in all directions from the centre.

This is part of the Dome of the Rock (see page 34). It is covered with colourful tiles.

IMAGE-FREE ZONE

You will not see pictures or models of people on mosques. Many **Muslims** believe that making pictures of people or animals is disrespectful to **Allah** (God). Other Muslims think it is all right to make paintings of great leaders and Islamic life. But most of these appear in non-religious books.

Beautiful rugs like these are on sale in bazaars throughout the Islamic Empires.

CHAPTER 4

THINGS TO DO

There are plenty of ways to keep busy in the Islamic Empires. You might like to watch or play some sport. Polo is a fast and exciting game. It is played on horseback. Wrestling is also popular here. Or you could go shopping at the **bazaars**. These are busy and colourful markets.

At the end of a tiring day there are many ways to relax. Join some local people for a game of chess. Listen to a musician or to a storyteller. You may hear tales of great battles and faraway places.

SPORTS AND GAMES

In the Islamic Empires, young men are encouraged to take part in sports. It helps make them good leaders and warriors.

Rulers and wealthy men may go horse racing or play polo (see picture below). They also do archery. Archery is the sport of shooting with bows and arrows. Others go hunting with falcons. These birds are trained to hunt animals for humans.

These men are playing a game of polo. There are two teams of riders.

Ordinary people don't have the time or money to do these things. But they might watch cock fights and ram fights.

RACING AND POLO

Racing is probably the most popular sport. There's horse racing and boat racing. There's even camel racing. Horse racing is good training for war. This is because battles are often fought on horseback.

The game of polo was invented in the Islamic world. It is played on horseback. Riders use a long mallet, or hammer, to hit the ball.

PLAYING CHESS

Chess is all the rage in the Islamic Empires. The **Muslims** learned it from the people of Persia (see map on page 5).

WAR GAME!

In the Islamic Empires, people thought that chess was good practice for war. They thought it helped people work out plans for fighting.

MUSIC AND STORYTELLING

Music and storytelling are very popular throughout the Islamic Empires. Some of the musical entertainment is religious. Some is local folk music.

There is folk dancing too. There are dances that celebrate fighting skills, such as the Arabian sword dance. Others celebrate harvests (gathering in the crops) or the changing seasons.

Caliphs (leaders) have musicians and dancers to entertain them. Favourite instruments include the oud and the ney. The oud is a four-stringed instrument. The ney is a long cane flute.

This picture shows musicians playing instruments. They are playing at a royal wedding.

ENTERTAINMENT RULES

Dancing is allowed in many parts of the Islamic Empires. But men and women must not dance together.

These people are from modern-day Saudi Arabia. They are performing the ancient sword dance.

STORIES AND BOOKS

Poets and storytellers entertain people on the streets and in dining halls. Their tales are full of excitement and romance.

You can also buy your own books here. **Muslims** learned how to make paper from the Chinese. The city of Baghdad has more than 100 paper shops and bookshops. Also, Islamic libraries have thousands of books. Libraries here are much bigger than the ones in Europe at this time.

SHOPPING

If you like shopping, you'll love the **bazaars** of the Islamic Empires. Bazaars are busy marketplaces with shops and stalls. They are packed full of lovely things.

Before going shopping, make sure you have the right type of money. For large purchases you'll need dinars. These are coins made with gold. Smaller coins include the silver dirhem and the copper fals.

These are coins of the Islamic Empires. They are marked with the place and the year they were made.

WOVEN GOODS

People here are very skilled at weaving rugs and blankets. **Nomads** are travelling people. They need rugs and cushions to sit on in their tents. When they pray, people have mats to kneel on. These are called prayer mats.

JEWELLERY AND POTTERY

The jewellery worn by the nomads makes lovely gifts. You can buy all kinds of silver jewellery. You can also find beautiful objects made from metals such as bronze, copper, or gold.

Some stalls sell pottery. They may sell pottery tiles, dishes, or pots. Some of the pottery is decorated with **calligraphy** (see page 36).

This little deer comes from Cordoba in Spain. It was made more than 1,000 years ago.

This is the Great Mosque and Hospital of Divrigi in Turkey. It was built more than 750 years ago.

CHAPTER 5

HEALTH AND SAFETY

The Islamic Empires are cleaner and healthier than most other parts of the world. But there are some deadly diseases about. Many of them are diseases we don't have to worry about in modern times.

Caliphs (rulers) keep the roads safe for travellers. They want to make sure that **Muslims** can travel safely to **Mecca** (see page 13). But this is also a violent time. You could find yourself in danger if you don't know the rules.

HEALTH AND HYGIENE

The **Prophet Muhammad** taught that it was important to keep clean. Because of this, the Islamic Empires are cleaner and healthier than many other places at this time.

Most houses have drains to take away dirty water. There are public bath houses. These are called **hammams**. Everyone can afford to bathe regularly at the hammams.

This picture shows the inside of a typical public bath house. ↙

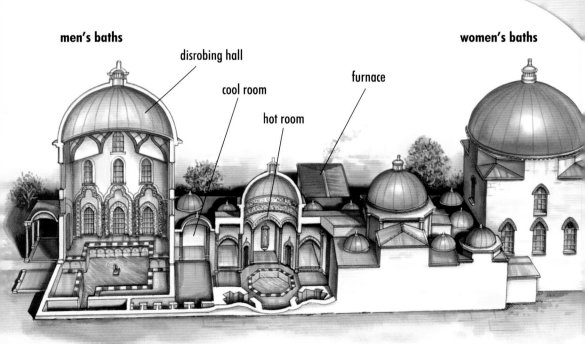

men's baths

disrobing hall

cool room

hot room

furnace

women's baths

VISITING A HAMMAM

Here are a few things you need to know before you visit a hammam:

- Most hammams have separate sections for men and women. If not, men and women visit at different times of day.

- Women may take all their clothes off. But men should wear towels around their waists.

- There are usually three rooms. The hot room has a marble table. This is where you can get a massage. The warm room is for washing. The cool room is where you go to relax and drink tea.

The hammam is not just somewhere to wash. It is a place to meet people. You can talk and drink tea there. You can even get a haircut.

DOCTORS AND HOSPITALS

You'll find proper hospitals in the Islamic Empires. The doctors here are very clever. They understand the importance of cleanliness.

In some other parts of the world, hospital beds can be filthy. There may be six patients sharing one bed. Some of them might already be dead!

HOSPITAL CARE

Islamic rulers have built many fine hospitals. These hospitals are open all the time. They treat everyone for free. There are separate hospital wards for people with different diseases. This helps stop diseases from spreading.

Hospital staff are skilled in different areas of medicine. There are surgeons who perform operations. There are doctors who are skilled at setting bones.

MOBILE HOSPITALS

In the Islamic Empires, there are medical teams that travel around on horseback. They carry medical equipment with them. These teams set up tents in villages to treat patients. They also follow armies into battle.

OPERATIONS

Islamic doctors use drugs to put their patients to sleep before an operation. They may give them opium or lettuce seed. In many other countries, patients are not so lucky. They have to stay awake and feel the pain.

This picture shows patients visiting an Islamic doctor. Doctors of the Islamic Empires were highly trained.

KEEPING SAFE

Islamic leaders have brought law and order to the empires. People who break laws are harshly punished. This makes it safer to travel than ever before.

Here are some of the punishments for law-breaking.
- Highway robbery (robbing travellers) – execution, or right hand and left foot cut off
- Theft – right hand cut off
- Drinking alcohol – 80 lashes with a whip.

DANGEROUS WORDS

Be careful what you say. A **caliph** (ruler) can have you executed for saying something he doesn't like. With just a wave of his hand, he can have you put to death immediately. Caliphs have many spies. Their job is to make sure that everyone in the empires lives by the rules.

WORST WORDS

Never say anything that might be thought insulting to **Allah** (God) or **Islam**. This is known as blasphemy. It is the worst crime you can commit in the Islamic Empires. Blasphemy is punished by death.

This picture shows a criminal being executed.
An officer called a vizier watches.

DHIMMIS

Some people do not want to become **Muslims**.
But they do want to be part of the Islamic Empires.
So they pay a tax (money) to the ruler. Then they
become dhimmis.

Becoming a dhimmi helps you stay safe. Dhimmis
have the same rights as Muslims. They are also
protected by the Islamic government.

These decorated walls are on the inside of the Friday **Mosque**. This is in the country of Iran. The building is now a museum.

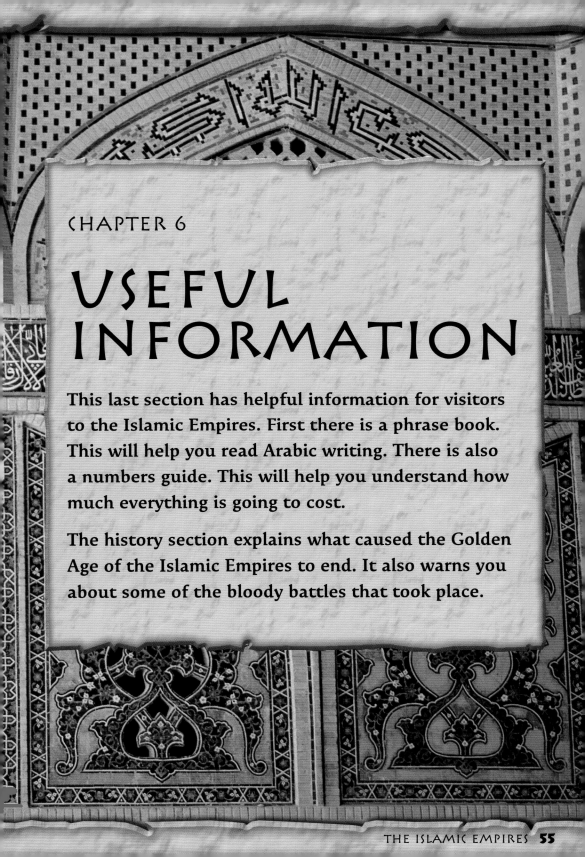

CHAPTER 6

USEFUL INFORMATION

This last section has helpful information for visitors to the Islamic Empires. First there is a phrase book. This will help you read Arabic writing. There is also a numbers guide. This will help you understand how much everything is going to cost.

The history section explains what caused the Golden Age of the Islamic Empires to end. It also warns you about some of the bloody battles that took place.

A	ﺍ
B	ﺏ
T	ﺕ
TH	ﺙ
J	ﺝ
H	ﺡ
KH	ﺥ
D	ﺩ
Z or DH	ﺫ
R	ﺭ
Z	ﺯ
S	ﺱ
SH	ﺵ
S	ﺹ
D	ﺽ
T	ﻁ
DH or Z	ﻅ
' or 3	ﻉ
GH	ﻍ
F	ﻑ
Q	ﻕ
K	ﻙ
L	ﻝ
M	ﻡ
N	ﻥ
H	ﻩ
W or U	ﻭ
Y or i	ﻱ

GETTING TO KNOW ARABIC

The Arabic language has spread across the Islamic world. People may also speak other languages. But with a little Arabic, everyone can understand each other.

USEFUL PHRASES

Here are some useful words and phrases. They are written as you say them in Arabic. They are not in Arabic symbols.

English	Pronunciation, or how to say it, in Arabic
Peace be upon you	As-salaamu 'aleykum
And upon you be peace...	Wa 'aleykum as-salaam
My name is...	Ana ismi...
What is your name?	Matha ismuka...
I want to buy...	Ana ureed an ashtiree...
I want to visit	Ana ureed an azoor...
I speak English	Ana Atakallum al-Injileeziya
How much?	Bikam?
That's expensive	Hatha ghaalee
Until we meet again	ila al-Liqa'

The Arabic alphabet has 28 symbols, or signs. These represent sounds and words. The symbols are written and read from right to left.

This Arabic writing says "As-salaamu 'aleykum". This means "Peace be upon you." Try writing it yourself. The arrows tell you in which direction you should move your pencil.

STANDARD NUMBERS

At the start of the Islamic Empires, people worked out sums in many different ways. Then about 1,200 years ago, travellers brought back a new system of writing numbers. This came from India.

The symbols changed slightly as people learned to write them. In time, the same form of numbers was used throughout the empires. It was also used in Europe and other parts of the world.

You'll recognize most of these numbers. But be careful. Numbers 2 and 3 might be on their sides. Also 4 and 5 are most unusual.

| 1 | 2 | 3 | 4 | 5 | 6 | 7 | 8 | 9 | 10 | about 1,000 years ago |

| 1 | 2 | 3 | 4 | 5 | 6 | 7 | 8 | 9 | about 700 years ago |

END OF THE GOLDEN AGE

The height of the Islamic Empires is called the Golden Age. The **Abbasid caliphs** were the last rulers of the Golden Age.

By the 12th century Abbasid rule had weakened. This was about 900 years ago. There were quarrels over religious differences. Some rulers were murdered.

THE CRUSADES

The empires were also weakened by the **crusades**. These were wars between Christians and Muslims. The First Crusade was fought in AD 1109. This was about 900 years ago. The wars continued for 200 years.

MONGOL ATTACK

In 1258, the **Mongols** destroyed the city of Baghdad. This was about 750 years ago. The Mongols were people from central Asia. Two million people were killed in the attack.

The Abbasid Empire never recovered. Law and order broke down in the empires. The Golden Age had ended.

LATER EMPIRES

You might decide to visit the Islamic Empires after the Golden Age. There will still be fascinating places to see. For example, you could see the great Mughal Empire of India. Or there's the Ottoman Empire based in Turkey.

This is one of the most famous Ottoman buildings. It is known as the Blue Mosque. You can see it in the city of Istanbul, in Turkey.

THE ISLAMIC EMPIRES AT A GLANCE

TIMELINE

AD 570	Birth of **Muhammad**.
610	Muhammad is given first messages from **Allah** (God).
622	Muhammad and his followers are forced out of the city of **Mecca**. They move to Madinah.
632	Death of Muhammad. Abu Bakr becomes the first **caliph** (leader).
634–644	**Muslim** armies invade Syria, Egypt, and Iraq.
638	Muslim soldiers take the city of Jerusalem.
644–650	Muslim armies invade Iran and Afghanistan. They also enter North Africa.
661	Muawiya becomes the first **Umayyad** ruler of the Islamic Empires.
750	The **Abbasids** take over from the Umayyads as rulers of the Islamic Empires.
762	The city of Baghdad becomes capital of the Islamic Empires.
836	Capital of Islamic Empires moves to the city of Samarra.
892	Capital of Islamic Empires moves back to Baghdad
969	**Fatimids** defeat Abbasids in Egypt.
973	Fatimid rulers make the city of Cairo, in Egypt, the Islamic Empires' capital.
1258	**Mongol** tribes (people from central Asia) attack Baghdad. Abbasid rule over the Islamic Empires ends.
1380s–1405	Mongols conquer much of central Asia, Iran, and Iraq.

1453	Ottomans capture the city of Constantinople. This is in modern-day Turkey. They rename the city Istanbul.
1501	The Safavids found their empire in Iran.
1556–1605	The first Mughal emperor rules in India.

FURTHER READING

BOOKS

Eyewitness Books: Islam, Philip Wilkinson (DK Publishing 2007)

History in Art: Islamic Empires, Nicola Barber (Raintree, 2005)

Islam (Atlas of World Faiths/Arcturus) by Cath Senker (Smart Apple Media, 2007)

Uncovering History: Everyday Life in the Ancient Arab and Islamic World, Nicola Barber (Smart Apple Media, 2005)

WEBSITES

- http://www.historyforkids.org/learn/islam/

- http://www.bbc.co.uk/religion/religions/islam/history

GLOSSARY

Abbasid series of caliphs and other leaders who ruled the second Islamic Empire. They ruled from 750 to 1258.

Allah Arabic word for God

bazaar marketplace with shops and stalls selling goods

caliph ruler and religious leader of a Muslim state or empire

calligraphy art of beautiful writing, especially in religious works

caravan long line of camels that travel across the Islamic Empires

caravanserai roadside inn where travellers can rest

crusade holy war

dhow ship with large triangular sails, used for trading

fasting going without food or drink

Fatimid series of caliphs and other leaders who ruled an Islamic Empire based in Cairo. They ruled from 909 to 1171.

halal Islamic religious laws about how food should be prepared

hammam public bath house

Islam religion based on the word of Allah, received by the Prophet Muhammad. It is also based on Muhammad's teachings.

Ka'bah square building in Mecca believed by Muslims to be the house Ibrahim built for God. It is the focus of Muslim worship.

madrassah religious school linked to a mosque

Mecca holiest Muslim city

Mongols tribe of people from the area of present-day Mongolia in central Asia

mosque place of Muslim worship

Muhammad founder of Islam. He is also known as the Prophet of God.

Muslim person who believes in Islam

nomad member of group of people with no fixed homes. Nomads move their animals between grazing places.

prophet someone who hears and passes on the word of God

Qur'an sacred or holy book of Islam

Ramadan month of fasting during hours of daylight

sultan king in the Islamic Empires

Umayyad series of caliphs and other leaders. They ruled the first Islamic Empire from 661 to 750.

INDEX